The Greatest Battles in History: The Battle of Trafalgar

By Charles River Editors

J.M.W. Turner's painting depicting the Battle of Trafalgar.

About Charles River Editors

Charles River Editors provides superior editing and original writing services across the digital publishing industry, with the expertise to create digital content for publishers across a vast range of subject matter. In addition to providing original digital content for third party publishers, we also republish civilization's greatest literary works, bringing them to new generations of readers via ebooks.

Introduction

Clarkson Frederick Stanfield's painting, *The Battle of Trafalgar*

The Battle of Trafalgar (October 21, 1805)

"May the Great God, whom I worship, grant to my Country and for the benefit of Europe in general a great and glorious victory; and may no misconduct in anyone tarnish it; and may humanity after Victory be the predominant feature of the British fleet. For myself, individually, I commit my life to Him who made me, and may His blessing light upon my endeavours for serving my Country faithfully. To Him I resign myself and the just cause which is entrusted to me to defend. Amen. Amen. Amen." - From the diary of Vice Admiral Horatio, Lord Nelson, on the eve of the battle.

The names of history's most famous battles still ring in our ears today, with their influence immediately understood by all. Marathon lent its name to the world's most famous race, but it also preserved Western civilization during the First Persian War. Saratoga, won by one of the colonists' most renowned war heroes before he became his nation's most vile traitor. Hastings ensured the Normans' success in England and changed the course of British history. Waterloo, which marked the reshaping of the European continent and Napoleon's doom, has now become part of the English lexicon. In Charles River Editors' Greatest Battles in History series, readers can get caught up to speed on history's greatest battles in the time it takes to finish a commute, while learning interesting facts long forgotten or never known.

Over the course of its history, England has engaged in an uncountable number of battles, but a select few have been celebrated like the Battle of Trafalgar, one of the most important naval battles in history. Before the battle, Napoleon still harbored dreams of sailing an invasion force across the English Channel and subduing England, but that would be dashed on October 21, 1805 by a British fleet that was outnumbered and outgunned.

That morning, Admiral Horatio Nelson's fleet, 27 strong, bore down on the Franco-Spanish fleet, approaching at right angles in two columns. French Admiral Pierre-Charles Villeneuve's disposition was conventional - a single line of battle, ill formed due to the very light winds and the poor seamanship of many of the crews. Traditional naval warfare strategies called for approaching an enemy fleet in one line and then creating a parallel line that allowed as many guns as possible to fire. At the same time, that kind of line of battle allowed for admirals to signal during battle, and it made retreating in an orderly fashion easier. After all, if an enemy's ships pursued during a retreat, they would break their own line. The problem with that strategy as Nelson saw it is that the ability to retreat meant fighting a decisive naval battle would be made much more difficult. Thus, at Trafalgar he employed a completely innovative strategy. The British plan was to punch straight through the enemy line with two approaching columns of ships, which would cut the Franco-Spanish fleet's line in three, prompting the melee that they knew would capitalize on their tactical superiority.

At 11.45 a.m. the *Victory* hoisted Nelson's famous signal: "England expects that every man will do his duty". While Nelson led one advancing column, the second column was led by Admiral Cuthbert Collingwood in the *Royal Sovereign*, and Collingwood told his officers, "Now, gentlemen, let us do something today which the world may talk of hereafter." By the time the Battle of Trafalgar was finished, Nelson had scored arguably the most decisive victory in the history of naval warfare. The British took 22 vessels of the Franco-Spanish fleet and lost none, but as fate would have it, the man most responsible for the victory in one of history's most famous naval battles did not get to enjoy his crowning experience. Nelson's tactics were bold and innovative, but they also unquestionably exposed the advancing column to merciless fire during the approach, especially the *Victory*, which was naturally at the head of the advance. Around 1:00, the *Victory* herself was locked in combat with the French ship *Redoubtable* when a sniper on the French ship's mizzentop took aim at Nelson from about 50 feet away. From such a distance, Nelson was an unquestionably conspicuous target, since he was impeccably dressed in his finest military attire. It was a habit that had caused great consternation before among his men, who had asked that he cover the stars on his uniform so that enemies wouldn't recognize his rank. Nevertheless, Nelson insisted on wearing them, famously countering, "In honour I gained them, and in honour I will die with them."

The impact of Trafalgar cannot be overstated, as it literally set the stage for the rest of the Napoleonic Era. Unable to invade England, Napoleon was limited to conducting war on the European continent, and while he spent the better part of a decade frustrating the British and their allies, he was eventually undone at Leipzig and then Waterloo nearly a decade after

Nelson's victory at Trafalgar.

The Greatest Battles in History: The Battle of Trafalgar comprehensively covers the entire campaign, analyzes the decisions made by the battle's most important leaders, and explains the aftermath of the British victory. Along with a bibliography, maps of the battle, and pictures of important people and places, you will learn about the Battle of Trafalgar like you never have before, in no time at all.

The Greatest Battles in History: The Battle of Trafalgar

About Charles River Editors

Introduction

Chapter 1: The Naval Campaigns of 1805

In December 1804, Napoleon had himself crowned Emperor of France at Notre Dame, adopting the title Napoleon I, and a few months later, Napoleon held another grand coronation in Milan to crown himself King of Italy. The newly anointed *Empereur* shook the European *ancien regime* to the core, and all across Europe, monarchs sat up and took notice. An upstart might become the leader of a country, but for him to declare himself royalty was unthinkable. Austria, Russia and Portugal eventually joined Britain in declaring war on France, but Napoleon remained focused on Britain itself. Napoleon believed that if he could defeat the British, Austria and Russia would lose heart and withdraw their armies.

Napoleon

Coronation of Napoleon I and Empress Josephine by Jacques-Louis David (1804).

With this plan in mind, Napoleon dispatched his navy southwards down the English Channel, attempting to persuade the Royal Navy that they were headed for the British West Indies, but even the French emperor couldn't have been confident when it came to naval maneuvers. By 1805, the British navy was the most powerful in the Mediterranean and the Eastern Atlantic, and they were actively enforcing the Continental Blockade.

Nelson

Portrait of Villeneuve

The British had been enforcing the blockade for several years by this point, which wasn't suited to Nelson's aggressive nature. When war had broken out in May 1803, Nelson was given a full command in the Mediterranean for the first time, and his flagship was the 100 gun *Victory*, with Thomas Hardy as captain. As ever, he sought battle with the hopes of annihilating the French fleet and thereby giving British interests a free hand. French naval strategy was more cautious, but it was essentially designed to secure supremacy over the English Channel, even if only temporarily, in order to facilitate Napoleon's intended invasion of Britain. In essence, this would involve uniting their Channel and Mediterranean fleets, whilst preventing a unified British fleet from intervening.

Hardy

Napoleon had devised a series of complex maneuvers and ruses designed to achieve this, but the problem was in the execution. He had little understanding of the difficulties of naval warfare, particularly in terms of communication and coordination. It was not possible to move fleets about on the map as if they were army corps, and moreover, most French admirals had a realistic if timid view of Britain's Royal Navy. Time after time, it was only the cajoling of the Emperor that would persuade them to sea, and even then they demonstrated a fondness for rapid retreats back to port. It would not be fair to caricature such conduct as cowardice, because commanders like Villeneuve appreciated that French fleets were expensive assets and difficult to replace.

Furthermore, as a nod to Nelson's abilities, the French naval officers operated cautiously under the belief that it was better to have a fleet than to expose it under anything other than very favorable odds. Years earlier, Horatio Nelson had comprehensively defeated the French Navy under Vice-Admiral Pierre-Charles Villeneuve at the Battle of the Nile in 1798. This had left the French fleet staggering, and perhaps just as importantly, its most senior naval officer now had a healthy fear of engaging Nelson in open battle again.

This protracted form of warfare did not suit Nelson's temperament, and yet he saw little opportunity for forcing the issue. By now, the Royal Navy was equipped and trained to maintain blockades on an indefinite basis, rotating ships, ensuring the crews remained sharp through competitive gunnery drills, and establishing a well organized system of replenishment. As a naval fighting force, its self-belief was matched only by its competence during the 18th and 19th centuries, and it fully expected to win any encounter on anything like equal terms with its enemies. At the same time, experienced Royal Navy officers realized the navy had no real means of forcing opponents to sea, making the type of decisive action Nelson sought very difficult.

In 1805, the Franco-Spanish had only a handful of harbors capable of sheltering a deep-sea battle fleet, including Toulon in the Mediterranean and Cadiz, Ferrol and Brest in the Atlantic. In early 1805, Admiral Villeneuve was blockaded in Toulon by Nelson with a large portion of the French fighting fleet, but Napoleon issued instructions for Villeneuve to force the blockade by any means possible before slipping past Gibraltar, after which he was to rendezvous with the Spanish fleet emerging from Ferrol and Cadiz. After a sortie into the Caribbean to attack British overseas holdings and persuade the Royal Navy to chase him across the Atlantic, Villeneuve was to double back towards the Channel, sweeping the depleted Channel Blockading Force aside and enabling the fleet in Brest, currently rotting at anchor, to set sail. Brest was to be the springboard for Napoleon's planned invasion of Britain, and it was currently full of warships and troop transports awaiting the embarkation of the vast army camped in nearby Boulogne, but the Royal Navy's stranglehold of the port meant that Napoleon's fleet would be blown to pieces if it tried to force its way out of the harbor. Thus, for the French plans to succeed, it was imperative that Brest be liberated, and for the British to prevent an all-out invasion of their home soil, which they were not nearly adequately prepared to resist (particularly with the Thames navigable virtually all the way to London), Napoleon's plans had to be frustrated at all costs. The most effective way to do this was to engage the French and Spanish in open battle on the high seas, where Nelson was certain he could succeed by dint of sheer superior seamanship, and end the threat once and for all by destroying the enemy fleet.

Despite his misgivings, Villeneuve eventually gave in to Napoleon's immense pressure. On January 16, 1805, Édouard Thomas Burgues de Missiessy, Villeneuve's colleague at Brest, managed to evade the blockade imposed by Rear Admiral Thomas Graves and escape into the Atlantic, bound for the West Indies. Another British fleet under Admiral Thomas Cochrane gave chase, and meanwhile Villeneuve slipped out of Toulon to join Missiessy. Nelson's blockade at Toulon was an "open" one, in which the heavy units lay back and leave the watch on the port to frigates. While the frigates reported to Nelson, Villeneuve actually returned to port only two days later; he had been defeated by appalling weather, which would have been difficult enough for his battleships to handle and downright impossible for his troop transports. Nelson did not know this, so he commenced a six week patrol of the western Mediterranean basin, swatting at phantoms. After nearly two years at sea, this did little to improve his mood.

While Nelson scoured the Mediterranean in the mistaken belief that Villeneuve was heading for Egypt, Villeneuve slipped through Gibraltar and then linked up with the Spanish before sailing for the Caribbean with Nelson in pursuit. Controversy still surrounds the purpose of the French sortie to the Caribbean. The British holdings there were vulnerable and vital, but Villeneuve had 7,000 troops embarked, enough to seize an island or two but not enough to make a difference in any invasion of Britain. Napoleon still had 90,000 troops on the Channel for that. It may simply have been a diversion to draw the Royal Navy away from the critical theater, but for Nelson, this was irrelevant. His task was to pursue the enemy and defeat him, so he pursued Villeneuve over to the Caribbean.

More frustration followed for both sides in the Caribbean. Villeneuve undertook little offensive action, while Nelson, usually one or two days behind, attempted to locate him and bring him to battle. False intelligence, simple bad luck and Villeneuve's timidity combined to prevent this from happening. On June 11, the French set off back across the Atlantic, with Nelson in pursuit as soon as he discovered what had happened. Misjudging French intentions, he sailed toward Gibraltar while Villeneuve went north.

Villeneuve was successful in evading Nelson's fleet in the Atlantic and was intent upon executing the second phase of Napoleon's plan, the attack on the blockading force off Brest, when he was ambushed by a Royal Navy squadron under Vice-Admiral Sir Robert Calder off Cape Finisterre in late July. Calder fought an indecisive action over the following two days, for which he was ultimately censured. Although two of the Spanish ships were captured, Villeneuve was allowed to make port in Ferol, joining up with other Spanish units there.

Nelson reached Gibraltar at the end of July. Disappointed, his Mediterranean fleet was merged with the Channel fleet and he took the *Victory* back to Britain. To his surprise, Nelson was given a rapturous reception wherever he went. He had, it was felt, saved the British West Indies and could do no wrong.

The third element in the French plan was Admiral Honoré Joseph Antoine Ganteaume, whose fleet was blockaded at Brest. Ganteaume attempted to break out in March, but when he was caught by a British squadron led by Vice Admiral John G. Cotton, he declined to fight and instead returned to port. Nelson had deliberately deployed his fleet well off the French coast, hoping to draw the enemy out, but this was an extremely difficult balancing act, for it made tracking the French more problematic: the looser the blockade, the more likely they were to slip through. This time it did not pay off. Although the French nearly ran into Nelson's fleet off Sardinia, they eventually managed to pass through the straits at Gibraltar and break out into the Atlantic. Followed by a Spanish squadron under Admiral Federico Carlos Gravina, they too headed for the West Indies.

Gravina

Furious at Villeneuve's timidity, Napoleon sent letters demanding that he sail for Brest without delay, and now that he was once again caught between a rock and a hard place, Villeneuve set sail in late March. However, he started seeing phantoms, so, becoming convinced the British fleet was shadowing his movements in preparation for an assault, he turned south and made berth in Cadiz with his fleet and a sizeable portion of the Spanish navy. 21 French ships of the line and a huge flotilla of transports remained immured inside Brest, useless, while Napoleon fumed and his army in Boulogne sat by their campfires and waited. With no sign of Villeneuve by late August, Napoleon was forced to march his army against his enemies in Europe rather than see its morale completely evaporate, thus scrapping, at least temporarily, his plans for an invasion of Britain.

With his fleets bottled up in Brest and Cadiz, Napoleon marched his *Grande Armee* towards Bavaria, where reports indicated a large Austrian army under General Karl Mack von Leiberich was headed. A Russian reinforcement army was not far behind Mack, but Napoleon marched his army between the two of them on October 9, cutting off Mack's line of advance and forcing him to fall back on Ulm. By separating the two Coalition forces, he was able to confront them piecemeal, and after a brilliant series of movements, Napoleon completely enveloped Mack's army and then utterly annihilated it on October 20th, 1805, killing or wounding 12,000 Austrians and capturing 30,000 more.

As it turned out, Napoleon won that decisive battle just a day before the Battle of Trafalgar was fought. Once Napoleon's army had moved, the British had begun the fleet movements that would bring about the decisive sea battle. Confident that the French fleet in Brest would be unable to put to sea if it met even scant opposition, the British admiralty detached 20 ships of the line and sent them south with the intention of engaging the French and Spanish fleets in Cadiz. Nelson, with his flagship HMS *Victory*, took control of this fleet in mid-August, and for weeks, the British fleet (numbering around 30 ships of the line) remained on station approximately 100 miles from Cadiz, with a loose daisy chain of light vessels, frigates and schooners keeping Nelson apprised of the enemy's movements and ready to notify him the second they left port.

After he had been given command of the British fleet assembled at Cadiz to watch Villeneuve, Nelson arrived in the *Victory* on September 27, and for a time, it seemed events would fall into an all too familiar pattern: the enemy seemed content to sit in port. Still, Nelson remained hopeful of a decisive encounter and planned accordingly. He had given considerable thought as to how he would fight such a battle, and he entertained his captains in a series of informal dinners aboard the *Victory*, during which plans were discussed and rehearsed. Nelson was not thinking in terms of a line of battle. He wanted a swirling melee.

Although Nelson's fleet at sea was experiencing supply problems due to their protracted time on station, this was nothing compared to the Franco-Spanish fleet's problems. Villeneuve and Admiral Gravina, his Spanish counterpart, were losing scores of men daily to illness and desertion and had several vessels severely understrength, with both nautical supplies and food dangerously low. Additionally, over the past several years the French fleet, manned mostly by conscripts, had spent most of its time blockaded in one harbor or the other and thus lacked professional sailors with seafaring experience. This meant that when the ships did put to sea, they were forced to practice rudimentary sailing maneuvers rather than gunnery, which made the crews much slower to fire than the British (a problem compounded by chronic powder shortages).

Villeneuve was so terrified of engaging Nelson that he called his captains to a vote on the matter, and his captains compounded his fears by agreeing with him. They decided the fleet would stay in port, but Napoleon was having none of it. He issued orders for Villeneuve to set sail immediately and make for Naples, where he was to disembark the contingent of French soldiers he carried as Marines to support operations there. If he met the British fleet and held the numerical advantage, he was to engage it immediately with all his strength. Any demurrals would incur the harshest consequences. Once again, Villeneuve had no choice but to put to sea, particularly as he had received information that a replacement was on his way.

Rather than face the disgrace of dismissal, on October 18th, Villeneuve issued orders for the combined Franco-Spanish fleet to set sail, despite the lack of favorable winds and fresh supplies and drafts for the ships. Nelson, waiting over the horizon for such a move, was immediately informed by his string of scout vessels that Villeneuve had put to sea. He signaled to his fleet to set all available sail and move to intercept the enemy. After months of waiting, Nelson would have his battle at last.

Chapter 2: 19th Century Warships and Naval Tactics

In the early 19th century, a prime warship was the aircraft carrier of its time and considered the pinnacle of 17th and 18th century engineering, industry and technology. Each warship was worth a vast sum, without even taking into account whatever cargo it might be carrying. If an enemy warship was captured, it would just as often as not be taken into service by the navy which had seized it, provided it was not unsalvageable (and the extent to which ships could be patched up, even with limited materials at sea, was truly remarkable). When this occurred, the navy (or private agents in the case of an enemy merchant vessel) would pay a bounty equivalent to the vessel's worth, known as prize money, to the crew which had captured it. Although the vast majority of this would go to the officers and the Captain in particular (with many captains becoming rich from prizes seized, particularly merchantmen with valuable cargo), every member of the crew stood to benefit. This led to an interesting tactical dichotomy; it made captains more risk-averse, since losing their ship would mean dishonor and humiliation at home, but it also made captains more enterprising, because the lure of vast wealth to be gained from the seizure of enemy ships often prompted desperate actions.

The warships of the day were classed depending on size and armaments into first, second, and third-rates. A first-rate would typically have 100 guns or more, a second-rate would have 98, while a third-rate could vary from 64-80 guns. At Trafalgar, the Royal Navy fielded 3 100-gun first-rates, 4 98-gun second-rates, one 80-gun third-rate, 16 74-gun third-rates, and 3 64-gun third-rates. By contrast, the Franco-Spanish fleet included 4 first-rates: one ship with 136 guns, two with 112 guns, and one with 100 guns. At the time, the *Santisima Trinidad* was the largest warship in the world. The fleet also had 6 80-gun third-rates, 22 74-gun third-rates, and one 64-gun third-rate.

Although warships, even under a full spread of sail (which was only employed rarely) appeared somewhat ungainly, with huge multi-decked hulls and a relatively small amount of mastage, they were still capable of reasonable speed; HMS *Victory*, for example, a 3500-ton craft, could manage 8-9 knots (around 9.3 miles per hour). By contrast, the *Cutty Sark*, built around 70 years later to be the very pinnacle of speed sailing, could manage 17 knots.

Depiction of the HMS *Victory* in Portsmouth

The HMS *Victory*'s starboard side

The defining characteristic of any warship, however, was not its speed, since battles were rarely fought in anything but light wind conditions and, at most, choppy seas. The most important aspect was the warship's guns. The HMS *Victory*'s 100 guns (104 if counting her 4 64-pound deck-mounted carronades) consisted of 30 32-pounders, 28 24-pounders, and 42 12-pounders (the pounds in question being the weight of the shots fired). This meant that the lightest gun on the *Victory* was equivalent to the heaviest field gun Napoleon or Wellington employed at Waterloo, and it carried more guns than an Artillery Division. If the *Victory*, which was significantly more lightly armed than some of the vessels of the Franco-Spanish fleet, fired its full complement of guns, the combined weight of shot would be in excess of 2,000 pounds. Given the sheer number and size of the artillery, it's unsurprising that no vessel would ever fire a "full broadside" (all guns on one side of the ship at once), because the concussion of this would likely tear the ship apart. Instead, they would fire in a rolling wave pattern. Regardless, this preponderance of guns was the reason why warships carried far more crew than would actually be needed to sail the vessel, as the sailors were needed not so much to rig and furl the sails and carry out maintenance aboard ship as they were to man the guns.

Naval guns predominantly fired iron solid shot, which the 32-pounders could propel up to 2,000 yards, but there were other munitions available in the naval captain's arsenal. This included grapeshot, which effectively turned the guns into giant shotguns and was used at close range, as well as chain shot, which consisted of two hollow halves of a cannonball joined together by a chain. Ships also fired bar shot, which was shaped much like a modern dumbbell. Both chain and bar shot were designed to wreak the maximum amount of havoc possible among an enemy ship's rigging, effectively leaving them dead in the water. British vessels, unlike their French and Spanish counterparts, also carried carronades, short-barreled cannons with a very wide mouth which were designed to fire a massive cannonball (sometimes fired with a cask of musket balls on top) as a deck-clearing anti-personnel weapon.

All naval guns, unlike their land counterparts, used a flintlock like a contemporary musket and a lanyard to fire, since having live flames aboard ship was considered far too dangerous. Indeed, fear of fire was a constant reality aboard vessels constructed entirely out of extremely flammable materials, especially when carrying on board vast quantities of gunpowder that even a stray spark might set off. It was not infrequent for an enemy vessel to offer the other assistance, even if they were embroiled in a battle, if it caught fire. This was practical if only because with the two ships fighting close together, flames were just as likely to destroy both vessels as one.

In addition to this, all vessels carried large caches of small arms. Each warship would have a full complement of Marines, armed with muskets and bayonets like conventional infantry, but in the event of a boarding action all sailors and officers would be expected to fight hand-to-hand as well. Ship-fighting was incredibly brutal, owing both to the close quarters of the action and the fact that it was effectively impossible to retreat at sea. In essence, the only options for the losing side were surrender or slaughter. Casualties could, and frequently did, run in excess of 50-60% of all hands killed or wounded, and the weapons employed reflected this. Rather than the slimmer swords and sabers of land forces, sailors employed heavy cutlasses with machete-like blades; tomahawk-like boarding axes; boarding pikes; a variety of firearms (including pistols, blunderbusses and muskets), and even rudimentary hand grenades (at the captain's discretion). The moment of boarding was usually incredibly brutal, carrying as it did the release from what might have been hours of incessant artillery bombardment, and entreaties for quarter were frequently ignored in the initial rush of bloodlust. Indeed, experienced sailors were known to lie low in expectation of defeat, only emerging from their boltholes and surrendering when the victors had calmed down.

Sea-fighting tactics were generally universal regardless of the navy's nationality, and they separated into two fairly distinct branches: bombardment and boarding. During the bombardment phase, the vessels would trade shots, with the advantage generally going to the ships which possessed the greater skill at gunnery both in terms of the speed of their broadsides and the ability of the individual gun captains to hit what they were aiming for. Although the cannons on the gundecks could not be swiveled from side to side since they had to fit through narrow gunports, their elevation could be altered, and it came down to the individual gun captains to judge, sometimes in heavy ocean swells, at which point their gun should fire to have the greatest chance of hitting the target. Traditionally, the guns would fire "on the uproll", when the vessel was being pushed upwards by a swell, allowing gunners to choose to aim their fire either at the hull of the enemy vessel or at its rigging. In this, Franco-Spanish tactics differed with the British. The allies preferred to "snipe" at enemy vessels at long range, firing a mixture of shot (including chain and bar) to destroy the enemy's sails and rigging and hopefully leave their vessels becalmed. By contrast, the British employed concentrated close-range gunnery to tear apart the insides of an enemy's hull, unseating guns, killing gun crews and battering a vessel so badly that it would be forced to surrender through sheer lack of men left to man its guns and rigging.

Firing at the waterline was also employed if the objective was to sink the vessel swiftly, but judging the precise target on this was difficult. Although ships could still be holed by a direct shot, they were thicker near the keel, and water immediately slowed cannon balls down to the point of rendering them harmless. Aim too high, and the shot would merely be shooting into one of the gundecks. Aim too low, and the shot would be entirely wasted.

The greatest fear for a captain in either scenario was to find himself "raked", being caught presenting his vulnerable bow or stern to an enemy who could then sail past and empty every gun of his broadside into it while being completely safe from retaliation save from the light guns mounted on the bow and stern. Because both bow and especially stern were vulnerable to enemy attack, being less solidly constructed than the sides, the shot would then scream across the entire length of the ship rather than straight through one side to the other, multiplying the potential for causing carnage exponentially and turning any piece of equipment or the ship itself into a cloud of additional murderous splinters and shrapnel. Being raked generally meant suffering enormous casualties, and while raking during a one-on-one duel could be chalked up to bad seamanship, full scale melees often put being raked outside of a captain's control.

In terms of fleet tactics for a bombardment, conventional wisdom dictated that two fleets deployed in line of battle horizontally and then sailed at one another from opposing quarters, like two trains heading in opposite directions passing each other. This served to prevent confusion, because the only way to communicate between vessels was via complex flag signals, which were almost impossible to discern in the chaos of battle once vast clouds of smoke obscured the battlefield and masts bearing flags could be easily shot away. The difficulties with communication also meant that it was relatively easy for an enemy force fearing defeat to disengage and flee, leaving a victory incomplete. At Trafalgar, Nelson devised his own revolutionary tactics to deal with these issues.

Boarding was even more straightforward. If two vessels drew so close as to be accidentally entangled in each others' rigging, or if one captain chose to deliberately lash the two together with grappling hooks and ropes, then what ensued was basically a land brawl on sea. During the action, marines and sailors posted in the rigging would fire upon the enemy decks with muskets or hurl grenades down into the opposing ship, while the gunners would fire a last salvo at their counterparts now literally feet away before running up to join the boarding party. Nelson also had different rules in this regard because he refused his captains' permission to place men in the rigging, claiming their fire risked setting the flammable linen sails alight. At Trafalgar, one French captain nearly succeeded in capturing the *Victory* itself by neglecting his guns almost completely and massing his marines and sailors on deck and in the rigging, letting the British batter his ship just for a chance to lay it alongside Nelson's vessel and overwhelm its crew by sheer numbers. It was a dangerous gamble which very nearly paid off, but it is indicative of the degree of tactical flexibility afforded to individual captains, who could, within the parameters of established seafaring wisdom, fight their ship and their crew in any way they saw fit to achieve victory.

Chapter 3: The Order of Battle at Trafalgar

Attached Vessels which did not participate in the battle are not listed.

Royal Navy

(Flagships in bold)

Name	Type	Guns
Victory	*First-Rate*	**100**
Britannia	*First-Rate*	**100**
Royal Sovereign	*First-Rate*	**100**
Temeraire	Second-Rate	98
Dreadnought	Second-Rate	98
Prince	Second-Rate	98
Neptune	Second-Rate	98
Conqueror	Third-Rate	74
Leviathan	Third-Rate	74

Minotaur	*Third-Rate*	74
Spartiate	*Third-Rate*	74
Orion	*Third-Rate*	74
Ajax	*Third-Rate*	74
Mars	*Third-Rate*	74
Tonnant	*Third-Rate*	80
Belleisle	*Third-Rate*	74
Achille	*Third-Rate*	74
Colossus	*Third-Rate*	74
Bellerophon	*Third-Rate*	74
Swiftsure	*Third-Rate*	74
Revenge	*Third-Rate*	74
Thunderer	*Third-Rate*	74
Defence	*Third-Rate*	74
Defiance	*Third-Rate*	74
Polyphemus	*Third-Rate*	64
Agamemnon	*Third-Rate*	64
Africa	*Third-Rate*	64

French Navy

(flagships in bold)

Name	Type	Guns
Bucentaure	*Third-Rate*	**80**
Formidable	*Third-Rate*	**80**
Neptune	Third-Rate	80
Indomptable	Third-Rate	80
Algesiras	*Third-Rate*	**74**
Scipion	Third-Rate	74
Mont Blanc	Third-Rate	74
Duguay Trouin	Third-Rate	74
Heros	Third-Rate	74
Redoubtable	Third-Rate	74
Intrepide	Third-Rate	74
Fougueux	Third-Rate	74
Aigle	Third-Rate	74
Pluton	Third-Rate	74
Algesiras	Third-Rate	74
Swiftsure	Third-Rate	74
Argonaute	Third-Rate	74
Berwick	Third-Rate	74
Achille	Third-Rate	74

Spanish Navy

(flagships in bold)

Name	Type	Guns
Nuestra Senora de la Santisima Trinidad	**First-Rate**	**136**
Principe de Asturias	**First-Rate**	**112**
Santa Ana	**First-Rate**	**112**
Rayo	*First-Rate*	100
Neptuno	*Third-Rate*	80
Argonauta	*Third-Rate*	80
San Agustin	*Third-Rate*	74
San Francisco de Asis	*Third-Rate*	74
San Justo	*Third-Rate*	74
Bahama	*Third-Rate*	74
Monarca	*Third-Rate*	74
Montanes	*Third-Rate*	74
San Juan Nepomuceno	*Third-Rate*	74
San Ildefonso	*Third-Rate*	74
San Leandro	*Third-Rate*	64

Chapter 4: The Battle of Trafalgar

William Lionel Wyllie's painting depicting Trafalgar

"During this momentous preparation, the human mind had ample time for meditation, for it was evident that the fate of England rested on this battle." – A British sailor at Trafalgar

On the morning of October 21st, 1805, the two fleets finally clashed off the Spanish coast near Cape Trafalgar. Villeneuve's combined fleet of 33 ships of the line had attempted to slip past the Royal Navy cordon, but Nelson's scout vessels had informed him rapidly of the enemy's movements, and he had quickly brought his fleet within striking range. On the eve of the battle, he had issued specific orders to his captains; instead of following the conventional strategy and deploying in line of battle alongside the enemy, Nelson's ships, divided into two columns, would drive straight at the enemy, attempting to head off the entire enemy battle-line and bisect it before engaging. The British plan was to punch straight through the enemy line with two approaching columns of ships, which would cut the Franco-Spanish fleet's line in three, prompting the melee that they figured they would capitalize on through their tactical superiority. In particular, Nelson planned to attack their command and control by isolating Villeneuve's flagship. The surrounded central section of the allied line would be overwhelmed by the attackers, while the vanguard would find it difficult to turn around and rejoin the fight. Another potential advantage created by Nelson's tactics was that it would bring the advancing British ships into the rear of the enemy line, allowing them to concentrate their fire on more defenseless ships in the rear while Villeneuve's line would have to attempt to turn itself around.

At the same time, this strategy was a major gamble. On the one hand, if it was successful, it would mean that all but the most nimble vessels on the very periphery of the enemy's line would be forced to engage and fight, resulting in a decisive battle. However, it also meant that the leading vessels of Nelson's two columns would risk being raked for the entire time they approached within range without being able to fire back except with their bow-chasers. This, in light wind conditions, could be a matter of many agonizing minutes. In making this decision, Nelson was counting on the enemy gunners' inexperience and the rough swells to make the impact of their long-distance firing negligible. In short, this was a gamble Nelson was prepared to take.

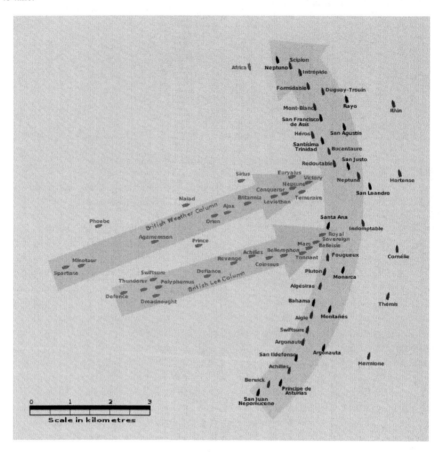

The dispositions at Trafalgar

Depiction of the battle lines at 1:00 p.m., just around the start of the fighting

While Nelson's advance was meticulous and precise, with he and his *Victory* and Vice-Admiral Cuthbert Collingwood, next in line of command, aboard his *Royal Sovereign* leading the two columns, Villeneuve's was a shambles. A combination of a series of contradictory orders to his captains both during the night and on the morning of the battle (including an order to about-face and head for Cadiz as soon as he spotted Nelson's ships) and gusting and contrary winds which made his inexperienced sailors struggle to carry out the correct maneuvers meant that Villeneuve's fleet was less in formation and more in a straggling, uneven, crescent-shaped line.

Collingwood

As the enemy sailed into view, Nelson had a chance for the first time to assess the strength of the Franco-Spanish fleet other than through the signals of his scout vessels. Despite the quality of his captains and their crews, the disparity in numbers between his fleet and the Franco-Spanish fleet was notable. Nelson could not know the enemy's exact numbers, but he could tell that his fleet had five less ships of the line and that at least three of the enemy far outgunned anything he could throw against them. As it turned out, Nelson's 17,000 sailors and marines were facing over 30,000 enemy combatants, and Nelson's 2,148 guns faced 2,568 Franco-Spanish guns. The enemy's superior numbers meant that by necessity, some of Nelson's captains would be fighting against two or even possibly three enemy ships by themselves. Nevertheless, Nelson was ready for this, and he had issued instructions during the night which left his captains a significant degree of leeway, knowing that in battle signaling would be virtually impossible. Nelson told them that he would not judge any captain who laid his ship alongside the enemy as having done wrong: "No captain can do very wrong if he places his ship alongside that of the enemy." Nelson's aggressive posture would serve to motivate his subordinates to attack however they could.

Nelson may have been history's greatest admiral, but even he once famously acknowledged that he "could not command winds or weather". On this day, the most difficult time for the British sailors was the approach. Given the very light winds and consequently slow speeds, the leading ships, including the *Victory*, had to endure over an hour of enemy fire on their bows before they could bring their own broadsides to bear. Nelson's calculation that French and Spanish gunnery would not be good enough to inflict serious damage before his two columns were in amongst them would be put to the test, and since the intended effect was to create a messy melee, Nelson had his ships painted a distinctly unique yellow and black pattern to help them identify each other.

At 11.45 a.m. the *Victory* hoisted Nelson's most famous signal: "England expects that every man will do his duty". According to his Flag Lieutenant John Pasco, the Admiral initially intended to signal, "Nelson confides [knows] that every man will do his duty." After considering that might seem to be too personal, he decided to change it again, as Pasco remembered: "His Lordship came to me on the poop, and after ordering certain signals to be made, about a quarter to noon, he said. 'Mr. Pasco, I wish to say to the fleet, ENGLAND CONFIDES THAT EVERY MAN WILL DO HIS DUTY:' and he added 'You must be quick, for I have one more to make which is for close action.' I replied, 'If your Lordship will permit me to substitute the confides for expects the signal will soon be completed, because the word expects is in the vocabulary, and confides must be spelt,' His Lordship replied, in haste, and with seeming satisfaction, 'That will do, Pasco, make it directly.' When it had been answered by a few ships in the Van, he ordered me to make the signal for close action, and to keep it up: accordingly, I hoisted No. 16 at the top-gallant mast-head, and there it remained until shot away." While Nelson led one advancing column, the second column was led by Collingwood in the *Royal Sovereign*, and Collingwood told his officers, "Now, gentlemen, let us do something today which the world may talk of hereafter."

Nelson's famous signal

From there, signal followed signal. Following his exhortation to his fleet, Nelson ordered his signaler to raise the flags for close action. The two British columns edged closer to the French line, and at noon, Villeneuve's *Bucentaure* gave the signal for his fleet to engage the British. For almost an hour, *Victory* and *Royal Sovereign* were under concerted bombardment by up to four enemy ships each, with *Héros, Santísima Trinidad, Redoubtable, Neptune* firing on the *Victory* and *Fougueux, Indomptable, San Justo* and *San Leandro* bombarding the *Royal Sovereign*. Nelson's tactics were bold and innovative, but they also unquestionably exposed the advancing column to merciless fire during the approach, especially the *Victory*. In short time, a cannon ball nearly cut Nelson's secretary, John Scott, in two, and Scott's replacement was also killed shortly thereafter. The *Victory's* wheel was shot away, forcing the ship to be steered below deck. Thomas Hardy was hit by a splinter near his feet, at which point Nelson mentioned to him "this is too warm work...to last long".

Ultimately, however, the British flagships suffered only relatively slight damage and casualties compared to the weight of fire that was poured upon them. *Belleisle,* the second ship in Collingwood's column, fared less well; though she suffered light casualties, the ship was completely dismasted and was thus forced to endure the enemy bombardment while dead in the water until she was rescued over half an hour later.

Around 12:45, after what must have seemed like an eternity to the sailors on board who were forced to endure the enemy bombardment without responding, the *Victory* and *Royal Sovereign* broke through the enemy line. *Victory* cut the line between *Bucentaure* and *Redoubtable*, firing a double broadside into *Bucentaure's* vulnerable stern and *Redoubtable's* prow. *Victory's* shot screamed down the entire length of both ships, wreaking carnage amid *Bucentaure's* packed gundecks. The broadside also severely damaged *Redoubtable*, but as noted earlier, *Redoubtable's* captain, Jean-Jacques Lucas, had massed most of his men on his deck and rigging in preparation for boarding.

Aboard the *Bucentaure*, Villeneuve was prepared to board the *Victory*, holding the ship's Eagle and telling his sailors, "I will throw it onto the enemy ship and we will take it back there!" However, a fluke of battle meant that *Victory* swung away from *Bucentaure*, attacking *Redoubtable* instead. Villeneuve's flagship would have to fight the advancing ships behind Nelson's *Victory* in the attacking column. Meanwhile, *Royal Sovereign* smashed through the line, driving past the Spanish flagship *Santa Ana* and raking it with a double-shotted broadside; since Collingwood's gunners had plenty of time to load their first salvo during the advance, Collingwood had instructed them to double-shot their guns.

What followed was a desperate and bloody melee. In the chaos of battle, ships were raked and raked again, with the smoke of the guns obscuring sight and the thundering sound making it impossible to hear orders, cries for help, and the screams of the wounded. Scores of men were killed by musketry, grenades, grapeshot, cannonballs and shrapnel, with hundreds more wounded. Some men went permanently deaf; and others were driven insane. In such conditions, the skill of the sailors made all the difference. Despite the British numerical disadvantage, not every French or Spanish captain was keen to get into the fight, especially those on the fringes who were actively looking to slip away or firing ineffectively from a distance. This meant that the allied flagships *Bucentaure* and *Santisima Trinidad* were trebled and even quadrupled by British ships.

Victory's gunners continued to fire into *Redoubtable's* hull, unseating her guns and tearing apart her middle decks, but this caused few casualties since the majority of Lucas's men had been massed upon the deck. Indeed, it was the men upon *Victory's* deck who suffered most, largely due to Nelson's order not to place marines or sailors armed with firearms in the rigging. By contrast, Lucas' rigging was teeming with sailors, who sniped with muskets and hurled grenades onto *Victory's* deck. It was one of these snipers that struck the blow which, had the British fleet not been so battle-hardened and competent, might well have turned the tide.

Around 1:00, the *Victory* was locked in combat with the *Redoubtable* when a sniper on the French ship's mizzentop took aim at Nelson from about 50 feet away. From such a distance,

Nelson was an unquestionably conspicuous target, since he was impeccably dressed in his finest military attire. It was a habit that had caused great consternation before among his men, who had asked that he cover the stars on his uniform so that enemies wouldn't recognize his rank. Nevertheless, Nelson insisted on wearing them, famously countering, "In honour I gained them, and in honour I will die with them." Indeed, Nelson had been the target of concentrated musketry throughout the engagement but refused to remove himself from his conspicuous position on the quarterdeck

Hardy was busy giving orders and directing men on the deck when he noticed that Nelson was no longer by his side. When he spotted Nelson, the admiral was kneeling on the deck. As Hardy ran over to him, Nelson simply stated, "Hardy, I do believe they have done it at last. My backbone is shot through." Nelson had been gravely wounded by a musket shot which entered his shoulder from above and passed through his spine. As Nelson was carried below deck, he hid his face so that his men would not see his predicament, and at the same time he continued to give orders. Once Nelson had been carried below deck to the surgeon, he told the surgeon, "You can do nothing for me. I have but a short time to live. My back is shot through." Nelson, who had lost an eye in battle years earlier, also allegedly declared "they have succeeded; I am dead". Although he lingered in agony for more than three hours, he would play no more part in the battle. He was carried below decks, where the surgeons on board gave what assistance and comfort they could.

Nelson is shot on the quarterdeck, painted by Denis Dighton circa 1825.

Nelson's dire straits were matched by those of his flagship, which was now firmly entangled with *Redoubtable*, and it was clear that Lucas intended to board with most of his men on his quarterdeck. *Victory*'s gunners had been summoned to repel boarders, but volleys of grenades from the French marines in the rigging had driven them to shelter. However, at the very moment when Lucas was preparing to storm across onto the *Victory*, *Temeraire*, following behind Nelson's flagship, nosed through the gap and, seeing the massed men above decks, unloaded on them with her 64 pound carronade, charged with solid shot and musket balls, from mere feet away. The effect was devastating, with almost the entirety of Lucas's boarding party wiped off the foredeck by the carronade. With his decks now a charnel house, Lucas tried to fight on, but his men were now outnumbered by British marines and sailors firing with muskets and carronades, and those who took shelter below decks were easy meat for the British gunners. Lucas and his men fought on with extraordinary bravery, but his gamble had failed. He was forced to surrender, having suffered 544 killed and wounded out of his original complement of 643, a staggering casualty rate of over 80%.

Meanwhile, other French and Spanish vessels were faring no better. Both *Bucentaure* and *Santisima Trinidad* were overwhelmed, raked, shot to pieces, and forced to strike their colors after hours of extremely vicious fighting. *Santisima Trinidad* was virtually shot to pieces, her large size less of an asset and more of a hindrance as she was unable to maneuver with any form of speed while the more nimble British third-rates could engage her from the angle most favorable to them.

Auguste Mayer's painting of *Bucentaure* being attacked by the *Temeraire*

Santisima Trinidad's situation could have easily been less dire if an allied vessel had come to her aid, but none did. The Franco-Spanish vanguard, which had formerly been the rearguard, had been spared from the fighting by the fact that the British column had cut the line behind them, but they merely fired a few broadsides at a distance before making off, leaving their comrades in the lurch. Still, despite their departure, the melee was an extremely hard-fought affair. Although the British lost no ships during the battle, some of them, especially *Bellerophon, Colossus, Royal Sovereign* and *Belleisle*, suffered appalling casualties of 25-30%. In a battle fought on land, that casualty rate would be more consistent with a beaten army than a victorious one.

However, the French fared even worse. *Santisima Trinidad, Argonauta* (both later scuttled by the British), *Swiftsure, Bucentaure, Aigle, Algesiras, Santa Ana, San Juan Nepomuceno, Monarca, Neptuno, San Ildefonso, Argonauta, Bahama, Fougueux, Intrepide, Berwick* and *Redoubtable* were all captured. *Intrepide* and *San Augustin* burned to the waterline after their flammable timbers and rigging were ignited by a stray spark, with the ships fighting them breaking off the attack to attempt to stay the blaze. When that proved futile, the British ships rescued the survivors, who took to their boats or cast themselves into the water to avoid the flames. One vessel, *Achille*, fared even worse, with an errant flame reaching the powder magazines and causing the entire ship to explode with most of the crew still on board. 85% of those aboard were killed, with only a handful managing to escape in boats or by diving or being flung into the sea by the explosion. *Fougueux* and *San Agustin*, both of which were raked more than once, also suffered appalling casualties (around 85% and 50% respectively). On average, the vast majority of ships engaged suffered 30-40% casualties.

Painting depicting the battle at 3:00 p.m.

As the battle raged above him, Nelson had continued to linger throughout the afternoon, tended to by people who tried to make him comfortable and give him lemonade and wine. Hardy came below deck to give him occasional updates, the final one informing Nelson that the British were on the verge of a great victory around 2:30, with French and Spanish ships striking their colors one by one. Ever the seaman, Nelson accurately surmised that there was a swell developing and asked Hardy to ensure that the British fleet was anchored. Around 4:30, about three hours after being shot, Nelson murmured, "Thank God I have done my duty." Chaplain Alexander Scott recorded that Nelson's last words were "God and my country", indicating that he may have been reciting his own pre-battle prayer, which he had written earlier that morning:

"Monday Octr 21st 1805

May the great God, whom I worship, grant to my country and for the benefit of Europe in general, a great and glorious victory: and may no misconduct, in any one, tarnish it: and may humanity after victory be the predominant feature in the British fleet.

For myself individually, I commit my life to Him who made me and may His blessing light upon my endeavours for serving my country faithfully.

To Him I resign myself and the just cause which is entrusted to me to defend.

Amen. Amen. Amen."

The prayer was later inscribed on oak timber from the *Victory*.

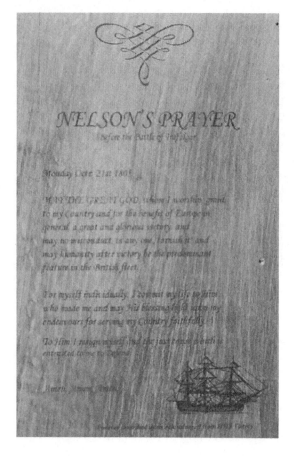

Nelson's prayer inscribed on an oak timber from the *Victory*

The Battle of Trafalgar ended with the remnants of the Franco-Spanish fleet which had not struck their colors in full flight for the safety of Cadiz. The British had lost 458 dead, including Nelson, and 1,208 wounded. The Franco-Spanish, by contrast, had lost 22 ships of the line captured, burned or destroyed, 2,343 dead, 2,543 wounded, and over 8,000 captured. The British lost two captains, George Duff and John Cooke, in addition to Nelson, while the Franco-Spanish had lost one Commander, five Captains, a Commodore, and two Admirals.

When King George III heard about Nelson's death, he reportedly broke into tears and exclaimed, "We have lost more than we have gained." *The Times* reported, "We do not know whether we should mourn or rejoice. The country has gained the most splendid and decisive Victory that has ever graced the naval annals of England; but it has been dearly purchased." Nelson's death aside, the Battle of Trafalgar was immensely important. Napoleon smashed the Austrians at Ulm and Austerlitz, presaging France's dominance of continental Europe, but he never again threatened Britain at sea. Trafalgar guaranteed that the Royal Navy remained the most powerful in the world for the next hundred years, buttressing a huge mercantile empire.

Chapter 5: The Aftermath of Trafalgar

An 1805 poster commemorating the Battle of Trafalgar

The events which marked the aftermath of the Battle of Trafalgar were, in many ways, as calamitous and dramatic as the battle itself. With all hope of victory lost, 15 Franco-Spanish ships of the line managed to make their escape, taking advantage of the fact that many British vessels were too battered by battle to give chase. Rear-Admiral Pierre Dumanoir le Pelley managed to slip away with four ships, including his flagship *Formidable* (80 guns) and *Scipion, Duguay Trouin* and *Mont Blanc*. This squadron of French vessels remained at large in the Gibraltar area for approximately two weeks before they were intercepted, defeated and captured by a Royal Navy squadron under Sir Richard Strachan. Of the 11 Franco-Spanish vessels which managed to limp into port under the command of the dying Admiral Gravina, only five were fit to take to sea again, thanks to a patchwork reassigning of men and materiel from other vessels.

However, those in port seriously questioned putting to sea and mounting a counterattack because in the meantime, a colossal storm had struck. The British ships, many of which were barely seaworthy themselves, had been forced to cast anchor, while the skeleton "prize crews" placed in charge of captured vessels (some of which were only staying afloat thanks to the herculean efforts of prisoners of war at the pumps) were in serious danger of seeing their ships founder and go down with all hands, including hundreds of prisoners locked up below decks. The storm was so bad that Collingwood, who had now taken over command in place of Nelson, would write later that November, "The condition of our own ships was such that it was very doubtful what would be their fate. Many a time I would have given the whole group of our capture, to ensure our own... I can only say that in my life I never saw such efforts as were made to save these ships, and would rather fight another battle than pass through such a week as followed it."

Thomas Buttersworth's painting depicting the storm after the battle.

One enterprising captain, Julien Cosmao, decided that the havoc being played upon the battered British fleet and their prizes by the storm might actually work to his advantage, so he ordered the refurbished Franco-Spanish flotilla, composed of *Pluton, Neptune, Indomptable, Rayo, San Francisco de Asis* and five light vessels, to take to sea. Collingwood ordered his captains to cast off the captured prize vessels they were towing, leaving them to fend for themselves, and shunted 10 of his men-of-war into a defensive line. Seeing the British present a united front and vessels still capable of fighting, the French and Spanish decided not to engage, particularly because the storm was mounting to a fever pitch and threatening their own vessels, with the wind raging to a full-blown gale and huge waves crashing over decks that were already weakened by cannon fire. However, the lighter and more agile support frigates following in the wake of Cosmao's squadron were able to use their superior maneuverability (and the fact they had not been engaged at all in the battle) to work their way past Collingwood's squadron and take two beleaguered British prize-crewed vessels in tow. These were the *Santa Ana* and the *Neptuno*, whose captured crews promptly rose up against their numerically inferior captors.

Cosmao

While the *Santa Ana* was successful in limping into Cadiz despite the storms, other vessels were not so fortunate. The coastline near Cadiz was incredibly treacherous, with shoals, sandflats and a vicious shoreline which lay to the lee of the storm. The *Neptuno,* despite being rescued, was wrecked off Rota, a fate which was shared two days of back-breaking struggle later by the *Indomptable,* which went down with over 1,000 sailors and marines on board, only 100 of which were rescued. Other ships, including those from the resurrected Franco-Spanish fleet, those taken as prizes by the British, or those that had escaped entirely, fared no better in the cataclysm, and it is a testament to the consummate seamanship of the British that they lost none of their weakened vessels on the lee shore.

The Franco-Spanish ships didn't do quite as well. *Rayo,* which had anchored close to the coast after the storm had torn down her weakened masts, was captured by *Donegal* (not part of

Nelson's original fleet) two days after the battle. Though a large portion of her crew was rescued, she sank, weakened by the storm, on October 26ᵗʰ. *San Francisco de Asis* was more fortunate; although wrecked, she was able to save the entirety of her crew. *San Agustin* managed to survive the storm, but she was in such dire condition that she was scuttled and burnt a week after the battle. *Santisima Trinidad,* which had been pummeled ruthlessly during the battle, foundered two days after in the storm, but the British were able to rescue the majority of her crew and prize crew. The crew of *Bucentaure,* Villeneuve's erstwhile flagship, took advantage of the chaos of the storm to rise up against the British prize-crew, but she had been so severely damaged by the storm that she was recaptured in a state of extremity two days later, sinking soon afterwards. *Redoubtable,* Captain Lucas' unfortunate vessel, shared a similar fate, rising up, being recaptured, and finally sinking on October 23ʳᵈ. Almost 200 men, mostly severely wounded casualties sheltering below decks, sank with the *Redoubtable. Fougueux* went down on October 22ⁿᵈ with all hands, killing over 502 French sailors, and *Aigle* shared a similar fate, sinking with over 300 on board. *Berwick* went down during the storm with over 600 men still on board, while *Intrepide* and *Monarca* were evacuated and then deliberately burnt in the storm's aftermath. *Algesiras* survived both the storm and the battle.

It has been alleged that the British were less than zealous in ensuring the survival of the enemy vessels, citing the disparity between Franco-Spanish vessels which foundered in the storm compared to none for the British, but this is an unfair assessment. The best argument against that accusation is that the British ships had generally fared better in the battle than their Franco-Spanish counterparts, and the state of their hulls, given the allied preference to aim for the rigging, was generally sounder. Additionally, the British could benefit from an almost full complement of prime seamen, whereas the Franco-Spanish ships had only a small prize crew to support them, and it was unreasonable to expect the prize crews to have freed the captive sailors in order to aid them. Moreover, even if the British displayed a callousness towards French and Spanish seamen (something belied by their behavior towards the crews of burning ships during the battle), at the very least one would expect them to undertake a significant effort to rescue their own prize crews who were managing the captured vessels. Furthermore, they stood to lose a significant monetary gain if the prize ships foundered.

As a result of the battle and the storm, almost every Franco-Spanish ship of the line that had put to sea under Villeneuve and after under Cosmao was destroyed. Admiral François Étienne de Rosily-Mesros, Villeneuve's replacement-to-be, arrived in Cadiz to find only five ships awaiting his command. They remained there, useless, until 1808, when Napoleon turned against his erstwhile ally and invaded Spain, at which point they were seized and pressed into Spanish service as British allies. Vice-Admiral Villeneuve, whose timidity and dithering played a significant role in the Franco-Spanish fleet's defeat, was taken to England as a prisoner. Eventually paroled, he returned to France where, in 1806, he was found dead in a tavern bedroom with six knife wounds to the chest. The official verdict for the unfortunate admiral's death was one of suicide.

Ironically, Villeneuve was on hand to witness Nelson's funeral back in England. After he had died, Nelson's body was placed in a cask of brandy mixed with camphor and myrrh and carried by the *Victory* to Gibraltar after the battle. Once there, Nelson's body was transferred to a coffin filled with spirits of wine, and then it was placed in another coffin made of wood salvaged from the mast of *L'Orient* after the Battle of the Nile. Nelson's body then lay in state in the Painted Hall at Greenwich for a handful of days before it was transported up river with a group of mourners, including Lord Hood and Sir Peter Parker. Nelson himself received an impressive state funeral in St. Paul's cathedral, and it was immediately evident that the process of transforming him into a national icon, something he had been keen to nurture himself, went into overdrive after his death, notably with the erection of the famous column in the centre of London, but also with a spate of hagiographies and poignant visual depictions of his final hours.

A painting depicting Nelson's coffin in the crossing of St Paul's during the funeral service, with the dome hung with captured French and Spanish flags.

Scott Pierre Nicolas Legrand's famous *Apotheosis of Nelson*, circa 1805–18. Nelson ascends into immortality as the Battle of Trafalgar rages in the background. He is supported by Neptune, while Fame holds a crown of stars as a symbol of immortality over Nelson's head. A grieving Britannia holds out her arms

Indeed, that process continues. In the BBC's 100 Greatest Britons program in 2002, Nelson was voted the 9th greatest Briton of all time. The bicentenary of the Battle of Trafalgar also touched off huge national celebrations under the banner of "Trafalgar 200". Over 200 years after his death, it's clear that contemporary Britons continue to hold Nelson in high esteem and associate with him everything that makes the British special.

Nelson's Column in Trafalgar Square, London

It's understandable that Nelson holds such a place in British history, because the Battle of Trafalgar is quite possibly the greatest sea battle in history. In terms of sheer scale, strategic significance, drama and brutality, it ranks alongside Actium, Lepanto and Midway, but there is a reason why one of the most important squares in London is named Trafalgar Square, and a reason why Nelson stands upon his column forever staring out towards that battlefield. Trafalgar was unprecedented in magnitude by any other naval action since the classical age, resulting in over 15,000 casualties and 22 ships captured or destroyed. It also left Britannia, as their previous anthem proudly proclaimed, to rule the waves.

In terms of strategic significance, Trafalgar was as momentous as Waterloo would be on land

10 years later. Not only did the resounding British victory completely free England from the threat of invasion by Bonaparte's fleet-borne armies, it also meant that their extended trade routes from the Caribbean or India were also protected from all interference save for American privateers. This allowed their vast trade empire to continue to accumulate the wealth and raw materials that drove forward both the British fleet and army and subsidized their continental allies, most notably the Portuguese. It also allowed Britain to enact with impunity their Continental Blockade, the great plan which throttled all French seaborne imports from their overseas colonies and left them to rely on what raw materials they could harvest within the confines of Europe. This affected not just luxury goods, such as sugar (for which the French were forced to cultivate sugar beets rather than employing cane), but also strategically vital items such as saltpeter, a necessary component in gunpowder. This meant that the French experienced a chronic shortage of cartridges for training, forcing them to train "dry", and it also affected the overall quality of the product, which was far inferior to the British equivalent.

Trafalgar, like Waterloo, bookended the struggle on land and sea between the British and the French during the Napoleonic Wars, a struggle which ultimately saw the British victorious on both counts. But while Waterloo remains more famous, and arguably the most famous land battle in history, in some ways Trafalgar had more long-lasting consequences. Without the safety upon the seas afforded by Nelson's crushing victory, the British would have been unable to harvest the far-flung resources of empire and turn the power of that wealth against the more powerful French, funding armies and allies capable of defeating Napoleon's veterans. Ultimately, in a post-industrial age, victory has inevitably gone to those capable of producing more materiel and manpower than the enemy, and Nelson's victory largely made that possible. Furthermore, Trafalgar was a colossal boost not just to British sea power but to the population's morale. It gave England a tragic hero in Nelson, who was already revered prior to his last, spectacular victory, and it rallied support for a war which many believed was unwinnable. True to the words of her anthem, Britannia did indeed rule the waves, and it continued to do so for decades after Napoleon and his dream of a French Empire had been destroyed for good.

Bibliography

Clayton, Tim; Craig, Phil. Trafalgar: The Men, the Battle, the Storm. Hodder & Stoughton.

Desbrière, Edouard, The Naval Campaign of 1805: Trafalgar, 1907, Paris. English translation by Constance Eastwick, 1933.

Fitchett H.W. (2011 e-book edition) Nelson and his Captains

Goodwin, P. (2002) Nelson's Ships: A History of the Vessels in Which he Served, 1771-1805.

Gardiner, Robert (2006). The campaign of Trafalgar, 1803–1805. Mercury Books.

Harbron, John D., Trafalgar and the Spanish Navy, 1988, London.

Harrison, J. (1806) The Life of Horatio, Lord Viscount Nelson of the Nile

Haythornthwaite P. and Younghusband W. (1993) Nelson's Navy

Howarth, David, Trafalgar: The Nelson Touch, 2003, Phoenix Press, ISBN 1-84212-717-9.

Kennedy, L. (2001 edition) Nelson and his Captains

Knight, R. (2005) The Pursuit of Victory

Lambert, A. (2010 e-book edition) Nelson: Britannia's God of War

Mahan, A.T. (1897) The Life of Nelson: The Embodiment of the Sea Power of Great Britain.

Rodger, N.A.M. (1986) The Wooden World

Warner, Oliver, Trafalgar. First published 1959 by Batsford – republished 1966 by Pan.

Warwick, Peter (2005). Voices from the Battle of Trafalgar. David & Charles Publishing.

Printed in Great Britain
by Amazon

21093739R00027